Economic Benefits to Local Communities from National Park Visitation, 2011

Natural Resource Report NPS/NRSS/ARD/NRR–2013/632

Yue Cui

Ed Mahoney

Teresa Herbowicz

Department of Community, Agriculture, Recreation and Resource Studies
Michigan State University
East Lansing, Michigan 48824-6446

February 2013

U.S. Department of the Interior
National Park Service
Natural Resource Stewardship and Science
Fort Collins, Colorado

The National Park Service Associate Director for Natural Resource Stewardship and Science office in Fort Collins, Colorado publishes a range of reports that address natural resource topics of interest and applicability to a broad audience in the National Park Service and others in natural resource management, including scientists, conservation and environmental constituencies, and the public.

The Natural Resource Report Series is used to disseminate high-priority, current natural resource management information with managerial application. The series targets a general, diverse audience, and may contain NPS policy considerations or address sensitive issues of management applicability.

All manuscripts in the series receive the appropriate level of peer review to ensure that the information is scientifically credible, technically accurate, appropriately written for the intended audience, and designed and published in a professional manner.

This report received formal peer review by subject-matter experts who were not directly involved in the collection, analysis, or reporting of the data, and whose background and expertise put them on par technically and scientifically with the authors of the information.

Views, statements, findings, conclusions, recommendations, and data in this report do not necessarily reflect views and policies of the National Park Service, U.S. Department of the Interior. Mention of trade names or commercial products does not constitute endorsement or recommendation for use by the U.S. Government.

This report is available from the Environmental Quality Division (www.nature.nps.gov/socialscience/index.cfm) and the Natural Resource Publications Management website (http://www.nature.nps.gov/publications/nrpm/).

Please cite this publication as:

Cui, Yue, Mahoney, E. & Herbowicz, T. 2013. Economic benefits to local communities from national park visitation, 2011. Natural Resource Report NPS/NRSS/EQD/NRTR—2013/631. National Park Service, Fort Collins, Colorado.

Contents

Figures and Tables

Executive Summary

The National Park System received 278.9 million recreation visits in 2011. Park visitors spent $12.95 billion in local gateway regions (within roughly 60 miles of the park). Visitors staying overnight outside the park (in motels, hotels, cabins, and bed and breakfasts) accounted for 54.9% of the total spending. About half (48%) of the spending was for lodging and meals, 21.4% for gas and local transportation, 9.7% for recreation and entertainment, 8.1% for groceries, and 12.7% for other retail purchases.

The contribution of this park visitor spending to the national economy amounted to 251,600 jobs, $9.34 billion in labor income, and $16.50 billion in value added[1]. The direct effects of visitor spending are measured at the local level in gateway regions around national parks. Local economic impacts were estimated after excluding spending by park visitors from the local area (9.8% of the total spending). Combining local impacts across all parks yielded a total local impact (including direct and secondary effects) of 162,400 jobs, $4.58 billion in labor income, and $8.15 billion value added. The four local economic sectors most directly affected by non-local visitor spending are lodging, restaurants, retail trade, and recreation and entertainment. Their spending supported 45,200 jobs in restaurants and bars, 34,100 jobs in lodging sectors, 15,500 jobs in retail and wholesale trade, and 20,000 jobs in recreation and entertainment.

In this 2011 study, payroll impacts were not included due to the conversion to a new accounting system for the National Park Service, which prevented obtaining the required inputs for such analysis in time for publication.

---

[1] National estimates use multipliers for the U.S. economy.

Introduction

This report provides updated estimates of National Park Service (NPS) visitor spending for 2011 and estimates the economic impacts of visitor spending. Visitor spending and impacts are estimated using the Money Generation Model version 2 (MGM2) (Stynes *et al*. 2000) based on park visits (also called recreation visits) during the calendar year 2011, spending averages from park visitor surveys, and local-area and national-level economic multipliers.

Visitor spending effects are estimated for all park units with visitation data. Direct effects cover businesses selling goods and services directly to park visitors. Secondary effects include: indirect effects resulting from sales to backward-linked industries within the local region, and induced effects from household spending of income earned directly or indirectly from visitor spending. Impacts of construction activity and park purchases of goods and services are not included.

Effects are estimated at both the national and local level. Most spending directly associated with park visits occurs in gateway regions around each park. Impacts of this spending on the local economies are estimated using local input-output models for each park. Local regions are defined as a 60-mile radius[2] around each park. To estimate impacts on the national economy, spending within roughly 60 miles of the park is applied to the national input-output model. System-wide totals covering impacts on local economies are also estimated by summing the spending and local impact estimates for all park units. Results for individual park units are reported in the Appendix.

2011 Updates

The 2011 estimates reflect new visitor surveys at four parks. In 2011, visitor surveys were conducted at Joshua Tree NP, Chiricahua NM, Fort Bowie NHS and Fort Stanwix NM.[3] Spending and visitor profiles for these parks were updated based upon the survey data. For other parks, spending profiles from 2010 were price-adjusted to 2011 using Bureau of Labor Statistics consumer price indices for each spending category. Consumer prices remained fairly stable between 2010 and 2011 except for an increase of 26% in gasoline prices and a 10% increase in transportation costs.

Visitor segment mixes were assumed to be unchanged except as reflected in overnight stays or new visitor surveys. Except for parks with new visitor surveys, average party sizes, lengths of stay and re-entry factors were assumed to be unchanged from 2010. Visit and overnight stay figures for all parks were updated to 2011 from the NPS public use statistics (Street 2012).

Multipliers for individual parks were estimated in 2011 based on 2008 IMPLAN data and IMPLAN's trade flow models (Stynes, 2011). Local regions were defined to include all counties within roughly 60 road miles of each park. For 2011, local region multipliers were adjusted from 2008 to 2010 based on structural changes in the national economy (i.e., ratios of jobs, income and value added to sales in each sector). Secondary effects and direct job ratios were adjusted to 2011 based on consumer price indices.

---

[2] The 60-mile radius is a general average representing the primary impact region around most parks. The radius is closer to 30 miles for parks in urban settings, and as large as 100 miles for some western parks. Economic multipliers are based on regions defined as groupings of counties to approximate a 60-mile radius of the park.
[3] These studies are conducted by the Visitor Services Project (VSP) at the University of Idaho. Reports for individual parks are available at their website: http://www.psu.uidaho.edu/vsp.reports.htm

Recreation Visits

The National Park System received 278.9 million recreation visits in 2011. Spending by visitors was estimated by dividing all visitors to each park into segments with distinct spending patterns and applying spending averages based on surveys of park visitors at selected parks. As spending averages are measured on a party-day basis (party nights for overnight trips), the NPS counts of recreation visits are converted from person entries to a park to party-days in the area by applying average party size, length of stay, and park re-entry factors. This eliminates some double counting of visits. To the extent possible, spending not directly related to a park visit is excluded.[4]

In 2011, there were 13.75 million recreation overnight stays in the parks. Twenty-nine percent of park visits were day trips by local residents, 40.0% were day trips from 60 miles or more,[5] and 27.7% involved an overnight stay near the park. Visitor spending depends on the number of days spent in the local area and the type of lodging for overnight trips. Day trips by non-local visitors accounted for 33.5% of the party days spent in the local area, day trips by local visitors, for 27.8%, and overnight stays, for 38.7%. Sixty-four percent of all overnight stays by park visitors were in hotels, motels, lodges, or bed and breakfasts outside the park; another 17.5% were in campgrounds outside the park, 7.5% in private homes; and 11.1% were inside the park in NPS campgrounds, lodges, or back-country sites resided in National Parks.

Visitor Spending

Visitor spending averages cover expenses within the local region, excluding park entry fees. Spending averages for each segment are derived from park visitor surveys at selected parks over the past ten years. Bureau of Labor Statistics price indices for each spending category are applied to adjust all spending to 2011 dollars.

NPS system-wide spending averages for 2011 are given in Table 1 for seven distinct visitor segments. A typical park visitor party of local residents on a day trip spends $49.86 and $75.02 if a non-local party (Table 1).

On a party-night basis, spending by visitors on overnight trips varied from $59.91 for back-country campers to $330.70 for visitors staying in park lodges. Campers spent $119.86 per night, if staying outside the park, and $86.72, if staying inside the park. Spending averages at individual parks varied from these system-wide averages due to differences in local prices and spending opportunities.

Table 1. National Park Visitor Spending in the Local Area by Segment, 2011 ($ per party per day/night)

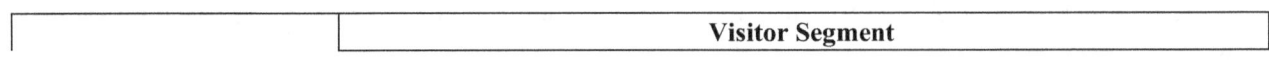

	Visitor Segment

---

[4] For example, spending during extended stays in an area while visiting relatives, on business, or when the park visit was not the primary trip purpose is excluded. For most historic sites and parks in urban areas, spending for one day or night is counted for each park entry. Where several park units are within a 60-mile radius, adjustments are made for those visiting more than one park on the same day.

[5] Day trips include pass-thru visitors not spending a night within 60 miles of the park, as well as stays with friends and relatives and in owned seasonal homes.

Spending category	Local Day Trip	Non-local Day Trip	NPS Lodge	NPS Camp Ground	NPS Back-country	Motel-Outside Park	Camp-Outside Park
Motel, hotel, B&B	-	-	151.89	0.31	5.25	92.67	0.12
Camping fees	-	-	0.39	15.30	2.44	0.11	25.16
Restaurants & bars	14.75	19.50	73.79	11.85	8.42	58.35	16.23
Recreation & entertainment	4.83	8.73	22.11	7.29	5.85	17.67	15.10
Groceries	7.27	7.14	12.56	14.63	6.43	14.39	12.36
Gas & oil	12.92	23.96	31.67	24.93	19.17	25.72	29.18
Local transportation	0.11	1.34	6.44	1.34	0.28	3.14	0.89
Retail purchases	9.97	14.34	31.85	11.07	12.07	27.08	20.82
Total	49.86	75.02	330.70	86.72	59.91	239.13	119.86

Note – Columns may not sum to totals due to rounding.

In total, park visitors spent $12.95 billion in the local region surrounding the parks in 2011.[6] Local residents accounted for 9.8% of this spending (Table 2). Visitors staying in motels and lodges outside the park accounted for 54.9% of the total spending, while non-local visitors on day trips contributed 20.5% of all spending.

Table 2. National Park Visitor Spending by Segment, 2011

Segment	Total Spending ($ Millions)	Percent of Spending
Local day trip	1,264	9.8%
Non-local day trip	2,659	20.5%
Lodge/cabin-in park	376	2.9%
Camp-in park	301	2.3%
NPS back-country campers	37	0.3%
Motel-outside park	7,105	54.9%
Camp-outside park	871	6.7%
Other overnight visitors [a]	339	2.6%
Total	12,952	100.0%

[a] Other overnight visitors include visitors staying overnight in the area but not incurring lodging costs.
Notes – Columns may not sum to totals due to rounding.

Expenses at lodging and restaurants/bars accounted for about a quarter of the spending, each. Expenses on transportation (mainly auto fuel) accounted for 21.4%, groceries 8.1%, other retail purchases 12.8%, and recreation and entertainment 9.7% (Figure 1).

---

[6] Spending figures exclude airfares and other trip spending beyond 60 miles of the park. Purchases of durable goods (boats, RVs) and major equipment are also excluded. Special expenses for commercial rafting trips, air overflights and other special activities are not fully captured for all parks.

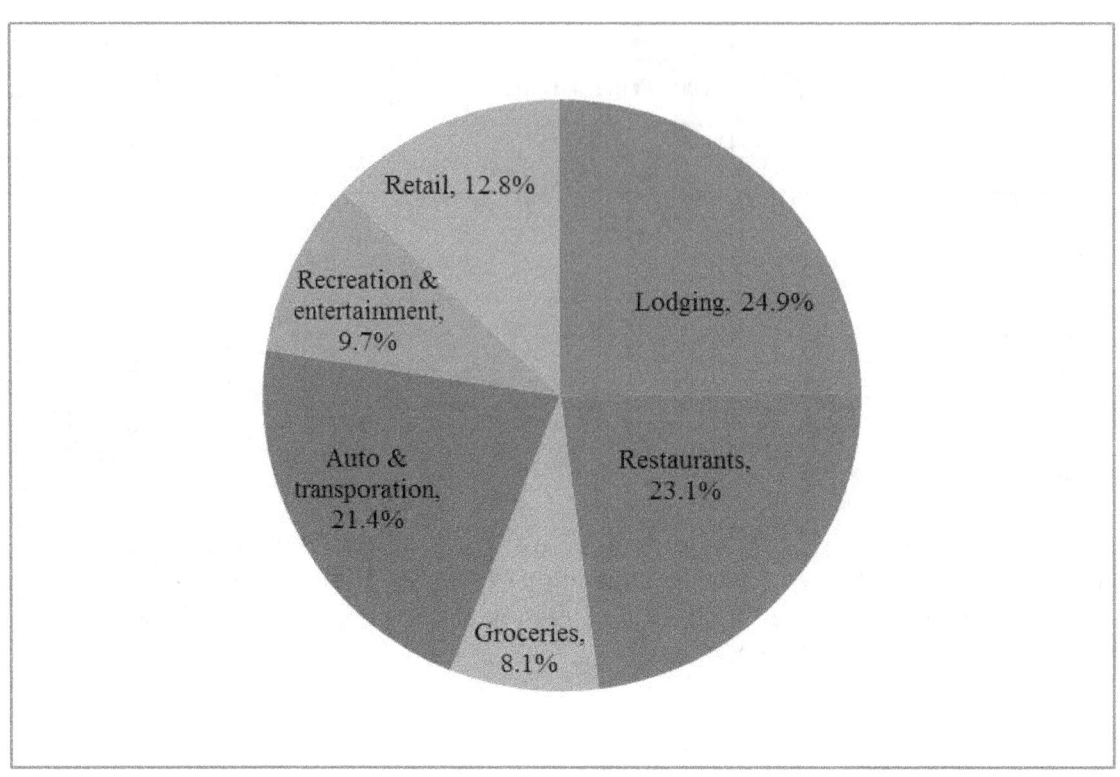

Figure1. Distribution of National Park Visitor Spending in 2011

Local Significance and Impacts of Visitor Spending

Local economic significance and economic impacts of visitor spending are estimated in the MGM2 model using multipliers for local areas around each park. Multipliers capture both the direct and secondary economic effects in gateway regions around the parks in terms of jobs, labor income, and value added. National totals are calculated as the sum of the local impacts for 374 park units that have counts of visitors.

Both economic significance and economic impacts were estimated for local areas. The average sales multiplier across all parks' local regions is 1.43. For every dollar of direct sales another $0.43 in sales is generated in the local region through secondary effects.

Economic Significance

The economic *significance* estimates in Table 3 measure the effects of all visitor spending ($12.95 billion), including that of local visitors.

The $12.95 billion spent by park visitors within 60 miles of the park in 2011 (Table 2) had a total economic effect (significance) of $14.99 billion in sales, $5.04 billion in labor income, and $8.94 billion in value added. Visitor spending supported about 177,500 jobs in gateway regions. Total effects may be divided between the direct effects that occur in local businesses selling goods and services directly to park visitors and secondary effects that result from the circulation of this money within the local economy.[7]

Table 3. Economic Significance of National Park Visitor Spending to Local Economies, 2011

Sector/Spending category	Sales ($ Millions)	Jobs	Labor Income ($ Millions)	Value Added ($ Millions)
Direct Effects				
Motel, hotel cabin or B&B	2,979	29,552	836	1,694
Camping fees	244	4,541	77	150
Restaurants & bars	2,991	51,435	1,089	1,653
Recreation & entertainment	1,255	22,331	418	784
Other vehicle expenses	173	2,009	88	102
Local transportation	315	6,522	158	242
Grocery stores	279	4,770	140	204
Gas stations	114	1,401	48	80
Other retail	583	10,500	273	423
Wholesale trade	266	1,570	114	206
Local manufacturing	537	685	48	118
Total Direct Effects	**9,736**	**135,316**	**3,289**	**5,656**
Secondary Effects	5,256	42,194	1,753	3,279
Total Effects	**14,992**	**177,510**	**5,042**	**8,935**

Notes: Economic significance covers all $12.95 billion in spending by park visitors in the local region, including that of local visitors. Columns may not sum to totals due to rounding.

---

[7] Secondary effects include indirect effects of businesses buying goods and services from backward-linked local firms and induced effects of household spending of their earnings.

Direct effects were $9.74 billion in sales, $3.29 billion in labor income, $5.66 billion in value added, and 135,300 jobs. The local regions captured 75.2% of all visitor spending as direct sales. Note that direct sales of $9.74 billion is less than the $12.95 billion in visitor spending as most of the manufacturing share of retail purchases (groceries, gas, sporting goods, souvenirs) is not included. It is assumed that most of the producer price of retail purchases immediately leaks out of the region to cover the cost of goods sold. Sales figures for retail and wholesale trade are the margins on retail purchases.

Economic Impacts

The economic *impacts* (which exclude spending by local visitors) in Table 4 measure the effects of the $11.69 billion spent by visitors who did not reside within the gateway regions.

Economic impact measures estimate the likely losses in economic activity to the region in the absence of the park. Should the park opportunities not be available, it is assumed that local residents would spend the money on other local activities, while visitors from outside the region would not have made a trip to the region.[8] Spending by local residents on visits to the park does not represent "new money" to the region and is therefore generally excluded when estimating impacts. Local resident spending is included in the economic significance measures, as these capture all economic activity associated with park visits, including local and non-local visitors.

Table 4. Economic Impacts of National Park Visitor Spending on Local Economies, 2011

Sector/Spending category	Sales ($ Millions)	Jobs	Labor Income ($ Millions)	Value Added ($ Millions)
Direct Effects				
Motel, hotel cabin or B&B	2,979	29,552	836	1,694
Camping fees	244	4,541	77	150
Restaurants & bars	2,616	45,161	951	1,444
Recreation & entertainment	1,122	20,033	375	701
Other vehicle expenses	158	1,843	81	93
Local transportation	312	6,451	156	240
Grocery stores	229	3,950	115	167
Gas stations	98	1,214	41	69
Other retail	502	9,072	234	363
Wholesale trade	220	1,314	93	170
Local manufacturing	417	539	37	91
Total Direct Effects	**8,897**	**123,670**	**2,996**	**5,182**
Secondary Effects	4,762	38,753	1,582	2,965
Total Effects	**13,659**	**162,423**	**4,578**	**8,147**

Note: Economic impacts cover the $11.69 billion spent by non-local visitors. Columns may not sum to totals due to rounding.

---

[8] To the extent possible, spending not directly associated with a park visit is also excluded. For example, only one night's expenses are counted for visitors in the area primarily on business, visiting relatives, or visiting other attractions. For parks with visitor surveys, spending attributed to a park visit was estimated based on the percentage of visitors identifying the park visit as the primary purpose of the trip.

Excluding $1.26 billion dollars spent by local visitors (Table 2) reduced the total spending to $11.69 billion for the impact analysis. Local visitors represented about 29.1% of all visits but less than 10% of all visitors' spending (Table 2). The total effects of visitor spending, excluding locals, was $13.66 billion in sales, $4.58 billion in labor income, $8.15 billion in value added, and 162,400 jobs. The economic sectors most directly affected by non-local visitors to the parks are lodging, restaurants, retail trade, and recreation and entertainment. Non-local visitor spending supported 45,200 jobs in restaurants and bars, 34,100 jobs in lodging sectors, 15,500 jobs in retail and wholesale trade, and 20,000 jobs in recreation and entertainment.

National Significance of Visitor Spending

The contribution of NPS visitor spending to the national economy can be estimated by applying the spending totals to multipliers for the national economy. This circulates spending that occurs within gateway regions around national parks within the broader national economy, capturing impacts on sectors that manufacture goods purchased by park visitors and additional secondary effects.

The estimates do not include park visitors' spending at home on durable goods such as camping, hunting and fishing equipment, recreation vehicles, boats, and other goods used on trips to the national parks. The estimates also exclude airfares and other en-route spending that occurs more than 60 miles from the park. Since many long-distance trips involve multiple purposes and often visits to multiple parks, it is difficult to capture these expenses without double counting or attributing spending not directly related to a national park visit.

With the above exclusions, the contribution of visitor spending to the national economy in 2011 was $30.09 billion in sales, 251,600 jobs, $9.34 billion in labor income, and $16.50 billion in value added (Table 5).

Table 5. Economic Significance of National Park Visitor Spending to National Economy, 2011

Sector/Spending category	Sales ($ Millions)	Jobs	Labor Income ($ Millions)	Value Added ($ Millions)
Direct Effects				
Motel, hotel, cabin or B&B	2,979	27,690	876	1,730
Camping fees	244	4,306	81	153
Restaurants & bars	2,991	52,937	1,059	1,628
Recreation & entertainment	1,255	22,153	418	785
Other vehicle expenses	173	1,996	90	103
Local transportation	315	6,492	175	250
Grocery stores	279	4,817	142	204
Gas stations	114	1,518	47	80
Other retail	583	10,510	276	425
Wholesale trade	468	2,637	205	365
Local manufacturing	2,858	4,121	291	711
Total Direct Effects	**12,259**	**139,177**	**3,660**	**6,434**
Secondary Effects	17,826	112,466	5,682	10,067
Total Effects	**30,085**	**251,643**	**9,342**	**16,501**

Note: Columns may not sum to totals due to rounding.

With the exception of manufacturing activity and a portion of activity in wholesale trade, the direct effects of visitor spending accrue to local regions around national parks.[9] Compared to the contribution to local economies (Table 3), an additional 74,100 jobs are supported nationally by NPS visitor spending, primarily due to the greater indirect and induced effects at the national level. The sales multiplier for NPS visitor spending at the national level is 2.51, compared to an average of 1.43 for local regions around national parks.

---

[9] Local economic ratios are therefore used to estimate the direct effects. National multipliers are used to estimate secondary effects. With the exception of wholesale trade and manufacturing sectors, the national direct effects (Table 5) are therefore the same as the local direct effects (Table 3).

State and Regional Impacts of Visitor Spending

Economic impacts of individual parks can be aggregated to the state level with a few complications. While most parks fall within a single state, there are 20 park units with facilities in more than one state. For these parks, shares of visits were assigned to each state based on percentages provided by the NPS Public Use Statistics Office. It was assumed that spending and economic impacts are proportional to where recreation visits are assigned.

Estimates of park visits, spending, and *state-level* economic impacts for each state and U.S. territory are given in Table A-2 in the Appendix. These state estimates are larger than the impacts for local economies since states generally include a larger economic productive capacity than local areas and therefore account for a larger share of the overall impacts.

Estimates of park visits, spending, and *regional-level* economic impacts for each NPS region are given in Table A-3 in the Appendix. Similar to the state-level impacts discussed above, these regional estimates are larger than the impacts for state economies since regions generally include a larger economic productive capacity than states and therefore account for a larger share of the overall impacts. As noted earlier, impacts reported here do not include long-distance travel, airfares, or purchases made at home for items that may be used on trips to national parks.

Methods

Spending and impacts were estimated using the MGM2 model. NPS public use statistics for calendar year 2011 provide estimates of the number of park visits and overnight stays at each park. For each park, recreation visits were allocated to the seven MGM2 segments,[10] converted to party days/nights spent in the local area and then multiplied by per-day spending averages for each segment. Spending and impact estimates for 2011 are made individually for each park unit and then summed to obtain national totals for impacts on local regions. Impacts on the national economy are also estimated by applying all visitor spending to multipliers for the national economy.

Spending averages cover all trip expenses within roughly 60 miles of the park. They therefore exclude most en route expenses on longer trips, as well as airfares and purchases made at home in preparation for the trip, including costs of durable goods and equipment. Spending averages vary from park to park based on the type of park and the regional setting (low, medium, or high spending area).

The segment mix is very important in estimating visitor spending, as spending varies considerably across the MGM2 segments. Segment shares are estimated based on park overnight stay data and, where available, park visitor surveys. For park units that lack recent visitor surveys, estimates are made by generalizing from studies at similar parks or based on manager or researcher judgment.

---

[10] Visits are classified as day trips by local visitors, day trips by non-local visitors, and overnight trips by visitors staying in campgrounds or hotels, lodges, cabins, and bed and breakfasts. For parks with lodging facilities within the park, visitors staying in park lodges, campgrounds, or back-country sites are distinguished from those staying outside the park in motels or non-NPS campgrounds. Visitors staying with friends or relatives, in owned seasonal homes, or passing through without a local overnight stay are generally treated as day trips.

For parks with VSP (Visitor Services Project) studies over the past ten years, spending averages are estimated from the visitor survey data collected at each park.[11] Averages estimated in the surveys were price-adjusted to 2011 using Bureau of Labor Statistics (BLS) price indices for each spending category. Sampling errors for the spending averages in VSP studies are generally 5–10% overall and can be as high as 20% for individual visitor segments (Stynes, 2011).

The observed spending patterns in park visitor studies are then used to estimate spending averages for other parks that lack visitor spending surveys. This procedure does not capture some spending variations attributable to unique characteristics of a given park or gateway region—for example, the wider use of public transportation at Alaska parks or extra expenses for special commercial attractions in or around some parks, such as rafting trips, air overflights, and other tours. When visitor studies are conducted at individual parks, these unique situations are taken into account.

Multipliers for local regions around national parks were applied to the visitor spending totals to translate spending into jobs, income, and value added and also to estimate secondary effects. All MGM2 multipliers were re-estimated in 2011 using IMPLAN ver 3.0 and 2008 economic data (Minnesota IMPLAN Group 2009). The multipliers were adjusted to 2011 based on structural changes in the national IMPLAN models between 2008 and 2010 and price changes between 2010 and 2011.

Based on national IMPLAN models, there were some significant structural changes in economic ratios and multipliers between 2008 and 2010. Most notable was a change in ratios for the recreation and entertainment sector (IMPLAN sector 410) due to under estimated output in 2008. IMPLAN ratios in 2010 for sector 410 were triple the 2008 estimates. Using 2008 multiplier would cause a significant underestimate of jobs, income and value added in the MGM2 recreation and entertainment sector estimates if the ratio were not adjusted from 2008 to 2010. The MGM2 estimates of jobs, income and value added are sensitive to any changes in these ratios and multipliers.

With the exception of parks with new visitor surveys in 2011, no changes were made in party sizes, lengths of stay, or re-entry factors between 2010 and 2011. MGM2 model parameters for individual parks are adjusted over time as new park visitor studies are conducted or other relevant information becomes available.

The retail margin used to the estimate economic impacts on gasoline sales with national park visits in 2010 was 22.3% and 8.3% at wholesale (Stynes, 2011). In a more recent report by Oil Price Information Service (2012), the retail margin is about 5% of the retail price. Energy Almanac (2012) shows that the distribution of gasoline, including retail and wholesale cost and profit, was approximately 10% of the gasoline's retail price, the refinery sector was 75% of the price, and fuel tax comprised 15% of the retail price in 2011. The fuel taxes can be shifted to the refinery sector since this shift has relatively minor effect on job estimates because the refinery sector has a very small job-to-sales ratio. In addition, U.S. refineries are concentrated in a few geographic areas and would seldom be located in NPS economic impact areas. As a result, the

---

[11] Detailed impact reports for parks that have included economic questions in their VSP studies are available at the MGM2 (http://mgm2impact.com/) or NPS social science websites (http://www.nature.nps.gov/socialscience/products.cfm#MGM2Reports).

gasoline margins used to estimate 2011 economic impacts of national parks were adjusted as follows: 90% went to the petroleum refining sector; 5%, to the wholesale trade sector; and 5%, to the retail sector. This 2011 adjustment reduced the estimation of local economic significance of spending on gasoline associated with national park visits by 5,800 jobs.

Spending and impact totals for states were developed from the 2011 estimates by summing the results for all units in a given state using the mailing address for the park to identify the state. Twenty parks have facilities in more than one state. For these parks, visitors and spending were allocated to individual states based on shares used by the NPS Public Use Statistics Office for allocating visits to states. For example, visits to Great Smoky Mountains NP were split 44% to North Carolina and 56% to Tennessee. It should be noted that these allocations may not fully account for where the spending and impacts occur. There are also many other parks with facilities in a single state but located within 60 miles of a state border. A portion of the spending and impacts for these parks may accrue to nearby states.

Errors and Limitations

The accuracy of the spending and impact estimates rests largely on the input data, namely (1) public use recreation visit and overnight stay data; (2) party size, length of stay, and park re-entry conversion factors; (3) visitor segment shares; (4) spending averages; and (5) local area multipliers.

Public use data provides reasonably accurate estimates of visitor entries for most parks. Some visitors may be missed by the counting procedures, while others may be counted multiple times when they re-enter a park more than once on a single trip. Accurate estimates of park re-entries, party sizes, and lengths of stay in the area are needed to convert park entries to the number of visitors or party days in the region. Visitors staying overnight outside the park pose significant problems as they tend to be the greatest spenders and may enter the park several times during their stay. Similarly, visitors staying inside the park may enter and leave it several times during their stay and be counted each time as a distinct visit. Re-entry factors adjust for these problems to the extent possible.

For multi-purpose trips, it is difficult to determine what portion of the spending should be attributed to the park visit. This is especially a problem for historic sites and parks in urban areas or parks in multiple-attraction destinations. For parks with visitor surveys, the proportion of days and spending counted was decided based on stated trip purposes and the importance of the park in generating the trip to the region.

Parkways and urban parks present special difficulties for economic impact analyses. These units have some of the highest number of visits while posing the most difficult problems for estimating visits, spending, and impacts. The majority of visits to these types of units were assumed to be day trips by local or non-local visitors, and only one night of spending was counted for overnight trips. Due to the high numbers of visits at these units, small changes in assumed spending averages or segment mixes can swing the spending estimates by substantial amounts.

Clusters of parks within a single 60-mile area pose additional difficulties. For example, the many monuments and parks in the Washington, D.C. area each count visitors separately. Similar difficulties exist for clusters of parks in Boston, New York, and San Francisco. To avoid double counting of spending across many national capital parks, we must know how many times a visitor has been counted at park units during a trip to the Washington, D.C., area. For parks in the National Capital Region, we currently assume an average of 1.7 park visits are counted for day trips by local visitors, 3.4 visits for day trips by non-local visitors, and 5.1 park visits on overnight trips. The total of non-local visitor spending for the National Capital Region in 2010 was $1.17 billion. This is 14% of the Travel Industry Association's tourist spending estimate of $8.3 billion for Washington, D.C., in 2008 (USTA 2010).

NPS units in Alaska also pose special problems for economic analysis. Spending opportunities near Alaska parks are limited and for many visitors the park visit is part of a cruise or guided tour, frequently purchased as a package. Most visitors are on extended trips to Alaska, making it difficult to allocate expenses to a particular park visit. Lodging, vehicle rentals, and air expenses frequently occur in Anchorage, many miles from the park. Also, many Alaska parks are only accessible by air or boat, so spending profiles estimated from visitor surveys at parks in the lower 48 states do not apply well. Due to the prominence of cruise lines and package tours, special studies are required to estimate the proportion of visitor spending that stays in the local regions around national park units in Alaska. In this report, Alaska statewide multipliers are used to estimate impacts for parks in Alaska.

A visit to one or more national parks is an important part of the trip for most Alaska visitors. One could therefore argue to count a substantial portion of tourism spending in Alaska as related to national park visits. The U.S. Travel Association estimated tourist spending in Alaska at $2.1 billion in 2008 (USTA 2010). This is ten times what we have included as spending by park visitors in the local regions around Alaska national parks. Including spending in Alaska outside the local regions would significantly increase the estimates; however, deciding which spending to include would be somewhat subjective.

References

Energy Almanac. 2012. The California Energy Almanac. Available at http://energyalmanac.ca.gov/gasoline/margins/index.php

Minnesota IMPLAN Group Inc. 2009. IMPLAN Pro Version 3.0, user's guide. Stillwater, Minnesota.

Oil Price Information Service. 2012. Public Company Rack-to-Retail Margins. Available at http://www.opisretail.com/images/press%20release%20images/BrandMargins%20FirstHalf.pdf

Street, B. 2012. Statistical abstract: 2011. Natural Resource Data Series NPS/NRSS/EQD/NRDS-2012/422. National Park Service, Fort Collins, Colorado.

Stynes, D.J. 2011. Economic benefits to local communities from national park visitation and payroll, 2009. Natural Resources Report NPS/NRPC/SSD/NRR –2011/281. National Park Service, Fort Collins, Colorado.

Stynes, D. J., D. B. Propst, W. H. Chang, and Y. Sun. 2000. Estimating regional economic impacts of park visitor spending: Money Generation Model Version 2 (MGM2). Department of Park, Recreation and Tourism Resources, Michigan State University, East Lansing, Michigan.

U.S. Travel Association (USTA). 2010. The power of travel, economic impact of travel and tourism. Available at http://www.poweroftravel.org/statistics/.

Appendices

Table A-1. Local-Level Impacts of NPS Visitor Spending on Local Economies by Park, 2011

Park Unit	Public Use Data		Visitor Spending 2011		Impacts of Non-local Visitor Spending		
	2011 Recreation Visits	2011 Overnight Stays	All Visitors ($000's)	Non-local Visitors ($000's)	Jobs	Labor Income ($000's)	Value Added ($000's)
Abraham Lincoln Birthplace NHP	163,568	-	6,061	5,636	94	2,566	4,334
Acadia NP	2,374,645	153,798	186,180	183,325	2,970	72,808	126,167
Adams NHP	219,975	-	15,139	14,076	172	6,911	11,458
African Burial Ground NM	108,585	-	7,407	6,866	77	3,715	6,165
Agate Fossil Beds NM	11,617	-	760	754	12	225	406
Alibates Flint Quarries NM	3,214	-	170	158	2	48	93
Allegheny Portage Railroad NHS	118,410	-	6,268	5,828	88	1,958	3,700
Amistad NRA	1,436,759	32,078	44,428	38,658	522	9,975	20,428
Andersonville NHS	108,812	-	4,032	3,749	57	1,284	2,456
Andrew Johnson NHS	52,322	-	2,770	2,575	41	1,028	1,838
Aniakchak NM & PRES	57	156	21	21	-	7	13
Antietam NB	384,987	-	20,018	17,996	243	8,813	15,021
*Apostle Islands NL	176,040	24,014	20,929	20,477	358	6,946	12,383
Appomattox Court House NHP	258,917	-	13,707	12,744	186	4,256	8,079
*Arches NP	1,040,758	50,915	113,722	113,722	1,638	33,855	65,849
Arkansas Post NMEM	37,127	-	1,376	1,279	20	350	645
Arlington House The R.E. Lee ME	576,816	-	39,697	36,910	396	15,681	26,077
Assateague Island NS	2,105,419	74,712	151,195	143,513	1,957	48,550	93,783
Aztec Ruins NM	41,106	-	1,380	1,337	17	392	736
*Badlands NP	870,741	44,576	22,203	22,203	317	7,302	12,064
Bandelier NM	193,914	9,300	9,218	8,908	135	3,461	5,941
Bent's Old Fort NHS	26,842	-	995	925	12	220	468
Bering Land Bridge NPRES	1,890	1,503	652	652	7	219	392
Big Bend NP	361,862	148,799	16,703	15,914	225	4,508	9,167
Big Cypress NPRES	941,393	19,957	117,467	114,919	1,891	66,660	111,384
Big Hole NB	36,290	-	1,345	1,250	19	376	709
Big South Fork NRRA	606,579	57,071	26,116	22,752	343	5,322	10,777
Big Thicket NPRES	137,722	1,891	9,891	9,382	138	4,755	8,248
Bighorn Canyon NRA	201,010	9,278	6,261	5,463	80	1,930	3,383
Biscayne NP	476,077	13,985	34,317	33,927	416	14,322	24,337
Black Canyon of the Gunnison NP	168,336	18,118	8,436	8,022	106	2,108	4,448
Blue Ridge PKWY	15,382,447	132,863	340,085	310,686	4,379	73,568	145,708
Bluestone NSR	41,670	-	1,901	1,660	24	542	938
Booker T. Washington NM	24,030	-	1,272	1,183	18	414	795
Boston African American NHS	379,906	-	26,145	24,310	298	11,936	19,788
Boston NHP	2,546,156	-	93,996	90,797	1,144	47,138	78,167
Brown v. Board of Education NHS	16,886	-	894	831	13	355	610
Bryce Canyon NP	1,296,000	133,221	115,066	113,928	1,726	32,695	64,683
Buck Island Reef NM	28,223	3,920	2,018	1,921	29	490	991
Buffalo NR	1,169,802	80,954	38,232	33,636	468	10,396	18,482
Cabrillo NM	813,351	-	55,975	52,045	681	22,071	39,667
Canaveral NS	1,005,001	3,146	72,256	68,525	1,034	32,487	57,312
Cane River Creole NHP	26,996	-	1,429	1,329	20	390	752
Canyon de Chelly NM	828,145	43,362	43,314	40,318	515	10,790	21,559
Canyonlands NP	473,773	87,910	39,976	39,571	519	12,526	23,338
Cape Cod NS	4,454,771	20,246	174,980	138,812	1,739	56,607	102,574

16

Table A-1. Local-Level Impacts of NPS Visitor Spending on Local Economies by Park, 2011 (continued)

Park Unit	Public Use Data		Visitor Spending 2011		Impacts of Non-local Visitor Spending		
	2011 Recreation Visits	2011 Overnight Stays	All Visitors ($000's)	Non-local Visitors ($000's)	Jobs	Labor Income ($000's)	Value Added ($000's)
Cape Hatteras NS	1,960,711	69,366	104,173	98,959	1,349	34,713	62,224
Cape Krusenstern NM	8,668	9,237	2,987	2,987	31	998	1,787
Cape Lookout NS	508,116	28,854	37,621	35,784	532	10,457	19,937
Capitol Reef NP	668,834	36,577	40,856	40,607	600	11,968	23,459
*Capulin Volcano NM	46,358	-	1,391	1,366	18	288	573
Carl Sandburg Home NHS	89,721	-	4,750	4,416	70	1,819	3,151
Carlsbad Caverns NP	365,000	107	21,256	20,720	299	5,771	10,646
Casa Grande Ruins NM	72,308	-	2,282	2,142	30	930	1,602
Castillo de San Marcos NM	741,042	-	50,999	47,418	590	16,962	30,206
Castle Clinton NM	3,985,366	-	81,538	56,980	571	23,915	39,008
Catoctin Mountain Park	264,460	29,348	14,393	13,459	143	5,623	9,347
Cedar Breaks NM	493,147	1,998	18,241	16,961	255	5,368	10,492
Chaco Culture NHP	39,175	14,990	1,111	1,072	14	306	536
Chamizal NMEM	113,817	-	7,833	7,283	110	2,747	5,260
Channel Islands NP	242,756	60,922	22,368	21,308	296	10,912	19,246
Charles Pinckney NHS	45,254	-	2,396	2,227	34	915	1,579
Chattahoochee River NRA	3,161,297	-	102,108	68,878	798	29,323	46,311
*Chesapeake & Ohio Canal NHP	3,937,504	7,690	54,008	33,909	435	16,885	28,105
Chickamauga & Chattanooga NMP	1,036,699	1,961	54,908	51,058	774	21,858	38,327
Chickasaw NRA	1,212,139	73,956	18,160	13,961	150	3,145	5,570
*Chiricahua NM	37,037	5,232	3,414	3,383	45	1,022	2,018
Christiansted NHS	119,335	-	4,422	4,112	62	1,039	2,087
City of Rocks NRES	95,764	-	6,887	6,531	93	2,089	3,815
Clara Barton NHS	15,620	-	1,075	999	11	425	706
*Colonial NHP	3,414,577	-	62,621	57,558	936	22,406	41,049
Colorado NM	435,460	15,188	23,251	21,657	295	6,732	13,242
Congaree NP	120,166	5,503	2,928	2,579	43	1,075	1,942
Coronado NMEM	153,042	-	5,671	5,273	75	1,934	3,552
Cowpens NB	223,923	4	11,854	11,022	176	4,385	7,836
*Crater Lake NP	423,551	79,054	34,688	33,665	549	12,781	24,037
*Craters of the Moon NM	198,545	14,119	6,821	6,746	81	1,748	2,940
Cumberland Gap NHP	828,947	14,887	44,029	40,973	602	10,475	20,889
Cumberland Island NS	74,279	16,961	5,270	5,025	73	2,236	3,959
Curecanti NRA	924,468	53,058	41,288	36,075	450	8,808	18,313
Cuyahoga Valley NP	2,161,185	5,539	51,473	37,248	530	14,931	24,305
*Dayton Aviation Heritage NHP	68,048	-	3,687	3,487	67	1,475	2,638
De Soto NMEM	355,653	-	24,476	22,758	347	11,143	19,676
Death Valley NP	946,867	224,379	50,240	48,087	616	16,114	30,619
Delaware Water Gap NRA	4,986,700	109,067	149,655	127,502	1,998	47,729	93,899
*Denali NP & PRES	406,582	109,047	160,010	160,010	2,669	69,258	111,362
Devils Postpile NM	97,207	4,215	3,642	3,394	41	1,028	1,961
Devils Tower NM	395,203	13,313	14,772	13,759	207	4,781	8,075
Dinosaur NM	213,559	40,066	7,671	7,159	92	2,080	3,992
Dry Tortugas NP	75,171	39,318	6,887	6,618	73	2,514	4,261
Edgar Allan Poe NHS	14,711	-	1,012	941	14	505	838

Table A-1. Local-Level Impacts of NPS Visitor Spending on Local Economies by Park, 2011 (continued)

| Park Unit | Public Use Data | | Visitor Spending 2011 | | Impacts of Non-local Visitor Spending | | |
	2011 Recreation Visits	2011 Overnight Stays	All Visitors ($000's)	Non-local Visitors ($000's)	Jobs	Labor Income ($000's)	Value Added ($000's)
*Effigy Mounds NM	82,581	-	5,124	4,901	82	1,278	2,547
*Eisenhower NHS	58,022	-	3,795	3,763	64	1,218	2,494
El Malpais NM	105,356	417	4,140	3,986	59	1,503	2,594
El Morro NM	48,332	1,943	1,816	1,738	23	365	787
Eleanor Roosevelt NHS	50,074	-	919	567	7	180	361
Eugene O'Neill NHS	2,593	-	178	166	2	89	153
*Everglades NP	934,351	28,868	146,784	141,069	2,336	83,242	140,066
Federal Hall NMEM	187,109	-	12,877	11,973	135	6,193	10,235
Fire Island NS	519,173	37,098	31,692	27,742	309	14,207	23,441
First Ladies NHS	8,254	-	568	528	9	189	341
Flight 93 NMEM	265,246	-	14,042	13,056	193	4,068	7,755
Florissant Fossil Beds NM	61,289	-	3,245	3,017	39	1,062	1,962
Ford's Theatre NHS	642,786	-	21,996	20,096	223	9,163	15,329
*Fort Bowie NHS	8,429	-	968	957	12	266	531
Fort Caroline NMEM	326,149	-	22,446	20,870	325	6,303	11,679
Fort Davis NHS	35,130	-	1,302	1,210	17	311	637
Fort Donelson NB	257,389	3	9,538	8,868	132	2,472	4,770
Fort Frederica NM	293,041	-	15,513	14,424	205	5,152	9,558
Fort Laramie NHS	52,916	-	1,961	1,823	27	534	988
*Fort Larned NHS	26,704	-	1,567	1,531	23	449	838
Fort Matanzas NM	570,695	-	39,275	36,518	454	13,063	23,262
Fort McHenry NM & HS	641,254	-	44,131	41,033	586	18,034	32,474
Fort Necessity NB	193,479	577	6,667	5,857	82	1,733	3,241
Fort Point NHS	1,338,508	-	92,117	85,649	1,145	45,382	78,273
Fort Pulaski NM	408,104	26	21,605	20,088	293	8,096	14,199
Fort Raleigh NHS	282,134	-	10,455	9,721	141	3,673	6,645
Fort Scott NHS	26,219	-	972	903	14	237	471
Fort Smith NHS	86,122	-	4,559	4,239	69	1,466	2,643
*Fort Stanwix NM	102,874	-	5,451	5,242	65	1,670	3,755
Fort Sumter NM	857,883	11	21,655	19,312	244	6,261	10,539
Fort Union NM	9,575	-	618	617	8	186	332
Fort Union Trading Post NHS	12,236	-	900	872	11	245	432
Fort Vancouver NHS	710,439	-	37,610	34,969	575	17,117	29,386
Fort Washington Park	409,381	-	14,009	12,799	142	5,836	9,763
Fossil Butte NM	16,552	-	783	783	10	205	397
Franklin Delano Roosevelt MEM	2,309,708	-	79,037	72,209	803	32,925	55,080
Frederick Douglass NHS	46,694	-	1,598	1,460	16	666	1,114
Frederick Law Olmsted NHS	4,022	-	277	257	3	126	209
Fredericksburg & Spotsylvania N	908,836	-	48,113	44,735	618	15,068	28,167
Friendship Hill NHS	30,039	-	2,067	1,922	29	634	1,196
Gates of the Arctic NP & PRES	11,623	6,576	4,008	4,008	42	1,343	2,410
Gateway NRA	7,697,727	8,165	150,947	60,712	668	30,724	50,537
Gauley River NRA	109,780	4,765	4,882	4,259	59	1,578	2,570
General Grant NMEM	104,769	-	7,210	6,704	76	3,468	5,731
George Rogers Clark NHP	145,596	-	7,708	7,167	111	1,856	3,676

18

Table A-1. Local-Level Impacts of NPS Visitor Spending on Local Economies by Park, 2011 (continued)

Park Unit	Public Use Data		Visitor Spending 2011		Impacts of Non-local Visitor Spending		
	2011 Recreation Visits	2011 Overnight Stays	All Visitors ($000's)	Non-local Visitors ($000's)	Jobs	Labor Income ($000's)	Value Added ($000's)
*George Washington Birthplace NM	130,647	-	3,569	3,275	44	871	1,696
George Washington Carver NM	30,787	-	547	519	7	145	272
George Washington MEM PKWY	7,417,397		34,370	5,021	50	1,886	3,084
*Gettysburg NMP	1,124,659	24,948	72,326	71,731	1,226	23,209	47,532
Gila Cliff Dwellings NM	25,317	-	716	690	10	161	312
Glacier Bay NP & PRES	431,986	34,309	4,592	4,592	59	1,765	3,169
Glacier NP	1,853,564	332,491	97,715	93,928	1,337	30,590	55,206
Glen Canyon NRA	2,270,817	1,311,741	233,895	233,895	2,755	88,152	138,044
Golden Gate NRA	14,567,487	60,927	289,700	119,573	1,566	62,428	107,537
*Golden Spike NHS	43,933	-	2,237	2,182	31	709	1,309
Governors Island NM	402,174	-	37,602	35,659	409	18,969	31,399
*Grand Canyon NP	4,298,178	1,357,679	467,257	467,257	7,361	194,112	346,447
Grand Portage NM	97,440	149	11,287	11,228	182	3,445	6,890
*Grand Teton NP	2,587,437	483,467	436,416	432,295	6,352	158,759	292,497
Grant-Kohrs Ranch NHS	20,293	-	752	699	11	253	444
Great Basin NP	91,451	36,026	4,528	4,339	56	1,029	2,096
Great Sand Dunes NP & PRES	280,058	46,830	10,770	10,096	134	2,636	5,289
Great Smoky Mountains NP	9,008,830	378,830	818,886	792,559	11,418	293,668	528,578
Greenbelt Park	190,427	24,507	13,539	12,671	134	5,279	8,776
Guadalupe Mountains NP	152,546	14,192	10,919	10,379	158	2,765	5,417
Guilford Courthouse NMP	346,617	12	18,350	17,061	281	7,312	12,746
Gulf Islands NS	5,501,872	138,680	164,709	95,972	1,264	30,575	57,097
Hagerman Fossil Beds NM	21,100	-	678	590	9	191	339
Haleakala NP	956,989	21,436	68,757	65,241	795	26,798	48,229
Hamilton Grange NMEM	7,817	-	533	496	6	266	441
Hampton NHS	32,165	-	2,214	2,058	29	905	1,629
Harpers Ferry NHP	255,348	-	9,993	9,117	135	3,963	6,955
Harry S Truman NHS	28,924	-	1,991	1,851	30	955	1,574
Hawaii Volcanoes NP	1,352,123	80,880	96,990	92,119	1,121	37,711	67,877
Herbert Hoover NHS	134,249	-	7,107	6,608	109	2,513	4,317
Home of Franklin D. Roosevelt NHS	125,488	-	2,723	2,392	29	778	1,577
*Homestead NM of America	69,845	-	2,308	2,161	32	654	1,166
Hopewell Culture NHP	33,834	-	1,254	1,166	18	326	611
Hopewell Furnace NHS	44,873	-	2,376	2,209	33	926	1,615
Horseshoe Bend NMP	65,892	-	3,488	3,243	49	980	1,776
Hot Springs NP	1,396,354	13,943	100,386	95,223	1,551	30,878	54,885
Hovenweep NM	25,858	1,558	1,390	1,297	17	403	740
Hubbell Trading Post NHS	88,231	-	4,671	4,343	57	921	2,109
Independence NHP	3,572,770	-	149,894	134,115	1,878	67,770	112,298
Indiana Dunes NL	1,840,513	22,823	58,817	41,251	572	13,892	24,596
Isle Royale NP	15,892	48,787	2,098	2,098	30	524	1,049
*James A. Garfield NHS	31,499	-	1,031	944	15	449	746
Jean Lafitte NHP & PRES	420,366	-	22,254	20,691	292	10,284	16,699
Jefferson NEM	2,259,020	-	97,764	85,939	1,110	44,057	75,918
Jewel Cave NM	77,146	-	4,084	3,797	60	1,319	2,260

Table A-1. Local-Level Impacts of NPS Visitor Spending on Local Economies by Park, 2011 (continued)

Park Unit	Public Use Data		Visitor Spending 2011		Impacts of Non-local Visitor Spending		
	2011 Recreation Visits	2011 Overnight Stays	All Visitors ($000's)	Non-local Visitors ($000's)	Jobs	Labor Income ($000's)	Value Added ($000's)
Jimmy Carter NHS	66,157	-	2,452	2,279	34	571	1,189
John D. Rockefeller, Jr. MEM PK	1,147,986	34,914	7,471	6,930	93	2,198	3,727
*John Day Fossil Beds NM	148,002	-	7,303	7,185	90	1,668	3,349
John F. Kennedy NHS	18,466	-	1,271	1,182	14	580	962
John Muir NHS	31,236	-	2,150	1,999	26	836	1,557
Johnstown Flood NMEM	105,906	-	6,356	5,870	97	2,161	4,092
*Joshua Tree NP	1,396,237	281,544	50,471	50,031	690	20,220	37,817
Kalaupapa NHP	57,841	-	3,062	2,847	34	1,142	2,049
Kaloko Honokohau NHP	162,906	-	8,624	8,019	96	3,215	5,771
*Katmai NP & PRES	48,939	8,239	12,583	12,445	166	4,928	8,847
Kenai Fjords NP	346,852	1,791	11,804	11,630	159	4,624	8,303
Kennesaw Mountain NBP	1,748,436	-	59,809	52,087	644	22,144	36,030
Kings Canyon NP	566,810	182,275	44,116	40,524	549	15,441	29,781
*Kings Mountain NMP	272,325	92	9,992	8,882	135	3,127	5,699
Klondike Gold Rush NHP Alaska	795,150	5,592	22,504	22,236	273	8,226	14,678
Klondike Gold Rush NHP Seattle	64,898	-	4,466	4,153	60	2,025	3,485
Knife River Indian Villages NHS	16,025	-	594	552	9	207	359
Kobuk Valley NP	11,485	9,715	3,955	3,955	41	1,318	2,354
Korean War Veterans Memorial	3,073,430	-	105,171	96,086	1,068	43,812	73,293
Lake Chelan NRA	43,827	10,595	1,803	1,646	23	827	1,414
Lake Clark NP & PRES	5,158	1,931	1,775	1,775	18	590	1,052
Lake Mead NRA	6,396,682	923,421	246,962	209,944	2,544	79,462	138,418
Lake Meredith NRA	734,030	17,098	32,446	28,237	382	8,189	15,636
Lake Roosevelt NRA	1,523,474	162,760	48,758	42,892	563	11,732	22,969
Lassen Volcanic NP	351,269	88,567	15,807	14,403	178	4,458	8,675
Lava Beds NM	124,113	10,827	4,678	4,456	52	1,187	2,319
LBJ Memorial Grove on the Potomc	239,058	-	16,452	15,297	164	6,499	10,807
Lewis & Clark NHP	191,867	-	10,157	9,444	142	2,386	4,794
Lincoln Boyhood NMEM	108,420	-	5,740	5,337	83	1,550	2,906
Lincoln Home NHS	296,214	-	16,367	16,061	233	6,006	11,410
Lincoln Memorial	5,971,220	-	204,331	186,680	2,075	85,120	142,397
Little Bighorn Battlefield NM	312,168	-	11,568	10,756	165	4,036	7,067
Little River Canyon NPRES	225,549	-	11,355	10,768	169	3,237	6,213
Little Rock Central High School NHS	66,106	-	3,500	3,254	52	1,479	2,389
Longfellow NHS	46,596	-	2,467	2,294	28	1,126	1,867
Lowell NHP	520,452	-	35,818	33,303	408	16,351	27,109
Lyndon B. Johnson NHP	100,056	-	6,886	6,402	90	2,718	4,738
Maggie L. Walker NHS	10,779	-	271	143	2	66	114
Mammoth Cave NP	483,319	78,172	33,504	31,618	508	11,080	19,822
Manassas NBP	659,740	-	9,669	9,256	105	3,558	5,776
*Manzanar NHS	79,587	-	8,434	8,381	92	2,091	4,286
Marsh-Billings-Rockefeller NHP	29,049	-	1,538	1,430	21	536	932
Martin Luther King Jr. Memorial	1,490,358	-	101,657	94,240	1,017	41,961	70,532
Martin Luther King, Jr. NHS	666,482	-	45,868	42,647	562	21,142	33,915
Martin Van Buren NHS	19,287	-	419	367	4	110	202

Table A-1. Local-Level Impacts of NPS Visitor Spending on Local Economies by Park, 2011 (continued)

Park Unit	Public Use Data		Visitor Spending 2011		Impacts of Non-local Visitor Spending		
	2011 Recreation Visits	2011 Overnight Stays	All Visitors ($000's)	Non-local Visitors ($000's)	Jobs	Labor Income ($000's)	Value Added ($000's)
Mary McLeod Bethune Council House NHS	18,142	-	621	567	6	259	433
Mesa Verde NP	572,329	70,891	43,382	41,397	551	12,518	24,207
Minute Man NHP	1,002,833	-	69,015	64,170	851	29,855	51,655
*Minuteman Missile NHS	59,389	-	4,229	4,229	65	1,467	2,505
Mississippi NRRA	99,398	-	11,029	10,567	186	5,981	10,155
Missouri NRR	179,983	-	9,061	8,593	140	2,204	4,171
Mojave NPRES	536,006	1,584	12,552	10,978	131	4,624	8,187
*Monocacy NB	36,674	-	2,796	2,591	33	1,299	2,122
Montezuma Castle NM	573,731	-	30,373	28,240	428	13,851	24,025
Moores Creek NB	58,118	252	2,150	1,999	31	704	1,293
Morristown NHP	222,395	-	11,773	10,947	123	5,662	9,358
*Mount Rainier NP	1,038,229	162,684	33,006	31,382	436	11,653	21,090
Mount Rushmore NMEM	2,081,722	-	74,365	69,991	1,007	22,080	37,100
Muir Woods NM	897,131	-	61,741	57,406	767	30,417	52,462
Natchez NHP	206,624	-	10,938	10,170	131	2,674	5,243
Natchez Trace PKWY	5,765,343	21,957	93,117	33,926	455	7,618	14,891
National Capital Parks Central	1,240,717	-	42,457	38,789	431	17,686	29,588
National Capital Parks East	1,167,393	-	39,947	36,497	406	16,641	27,839
National Park of American Samoa	8,716	-	744	713	11	188	381
Natural Bridges NM	91,184	6,665	4,918	4,590	59	1,191	2,339
Navajo NM	87,388	2,533	4,655	4,335	56	1,348	2,515
New Bedford Whaling NHP	273,862	-	14,250	13,618	207	6,140	11,616
New Orleans Jazz NHP	130,393	-	6,903	6,418	90	3,190	5,180
*New River Gorge NR	1,071,088	8,861	46,224	43,316	596	13,647	23,667
Nez Perce NHP	286,259	-	10,608	9,863	151	3,849	7,119
Nicodemus NHS	2,681	-	133	130	2	38	68
Ninety Six NHS	70,099	-	3,711	3,450	50	946	1,793
Niobrara NSR	65,785	-	3,312	3,141	51	806	1,525
Noatak NPRES	11,722	9,694	4,036	4,036	42	1,343	2,397
North Cascades NP	19,208	17,002	1,252	1,206	16	582	997
Obed W&SR	212,458	1,340	9,711	8,482	124	2,277	4,420
Ocmulgee NM	122,722	-	6,497	6,041	93	2,145	4,109
*Olympic NP	2,966,502	298,235	115,317	105,561	1,497	28,293	59,819
Oregon Caves NM	76,194	6,307	3,848	3,578	55	1,212	2,393
Organ Pipe Cactus NM	211,405	13,024	11,358	10,594	160	5,099	8,869
Ozark NSR	1,365,960	168,595	65,280	57,823	861	13,337	27,211
Padre Island NS	542,873	59,828	38,805	36,897	516	10,304	19,878
Palo Alto Battlefield NHP	24,752	-	917	853	13	303	593
Pea Ridge NMP	114,234	-	6,047	5,623	88	1,537	2,833
Pecos NHP	43,873	-	1,022	989	15	377	642
Pennsylvania Avenue NHS	236,136	-	8,080	7,382	82	3,366	5,631
*Perry's Victory & Intl. Peace M	93,119	1,581	7,422	7,422	147	3,430	6,037
Petersburg NB	213,261	-	11,290	10,497	155	3,799	7,139
Petrified Forest NP	614,054	4,611	44,161	41,879	568	11,735	23,317
Petroglyph NM	114,428	-	5,060	4,098	66	1,728	2,987

Table A-1. Local-Level Impacts of NPS Visitor Spending on Local Economies by Park, 2011 (continued)

Park Unit	Public Use Data		Visitor Spending 2011		Impacts of Non-local Visitor Spending		
	2011 Recreation Visits	2011 Overnight Stays	All Visitors ($000's)	Non-local Visitors ($000's)	Jobs	Labor Income ($000's)	Value Added ($000's)
*Pictured Rocks NL	561,104	33,974	24,970	24,532	357	5,676	12,414
Pinnacles NM	393,219	-	8,415	6,942	82	2,802	4,823
Pipe Spring NM	57,360	-	3,037	2,823	39	933	1,752
Pipestone NM	61,908	-	2,846	2,762	44	991	1,678
Piscataway Park	279,060	-	9,549	8,724	97	3,978	6,655
Point Reyes NS	2,129,116	40,822	93,317	84,981	1,105	43,524	75,171
Port Chicago Naval Magazine NM	545	-	37	34	1	21	36
President W.J. Clinton Birthplace	9,749	-	512	474	7	124	254
President's Park	786,151	-	26,902	24,578	273	11,207	18,748
Prince William Forest Park	379,535	48,504	21,833	16,328	172	6,494	10,808
Pu'uhonua o Honaunau NHP	426,224	-	22,564	20,980	252	8,412	15,099
Pu'ukohola Heiau NHS	133,306	-	7,057	6,562	79	2,631	4,722
Rainbow Bridge NM	92,311	-	4,887	4,544	60	1,485	2,701
Redwood NP	380,167	5,420	20,172	18,186	247	4,689	9,966
Richmond NBP	139,376	-	10,374	9,335	146	4,420	7,697
Rio Grande W&SR	873	4,871	106	105	1	22	45
River Raisin NBP	36,206	-	3,090	2,961	52	1,667	2,837
Rock Creek Park	2,050,490	-	70,166	64,105	713	29,230	48,899
Rocky Mountain NP	3,176,941	200,712	196,127	191,892	2,742	71,849	138,269
Roger Williams NMEM	50,909	-	3,504	3,258	46	1,420	2,459
Ross Lake NRA	728,353	71,820	23,339	20,516	280	9,832	16,804
Russell Cave NM	20,717	-	1,097	1,020	16	274	526
Sagamore Hill NHS	53,336	-	3,671	3,413	41	1,516	2,726
Saguaro NP	610,045	2,033	21,949	15,156	211	5,547	10,044
Saint Croix NSR	273,729	29,738	8,803	7,740	122	2,348	4,293
Saint Paul's Church NHS	14,926	-	1,027	955	11	494	816
*Saint-Gaudens NHS	32,695	-	1,297	1,193	19	494	869
Salem Maritime NHS	737,073	-	50,726	47,164	578	23,157	38,392
Salinas Pueblo Missions NM	29,786	-	823	792	12	306	520
Salt River Bay NHP & Ecological	2,419	-	206	198	3	52	106
San Antonio Missions NHP	568,021	-	23,831	21,323	297	8,913	15,385
San Francisco Maritime NHP	4,224,897	10,876	95,492	70,774	855	33,761	58,207
San Juan Island NHP	266,717	-	18,356	17,067	235	5,939	11,420
San Juan NHS	1,229,590	-	65,093	60,523	892	17,812	34,157
Sand Creek Massacre NHS	3,935	-	336	322	4	80	172
Santa Monica Mountains NRA	609,636	144	26,192	17,258	242	9,013	15,833
Saratoga NHP	65,043	-	2,410	2,241	27	700	1,426
Saugus Iron Works NHS	11,121	-	765	712	9	349	579
Scotts Bluff NM	128,811	-	4,416	3,586	60	1,134	2,033
*Sequoia NP	1,006,583	228,644	77,776	71,141	965	27,119	52,409
Shenandoah NP	1,209,883	282,888	73,908	65,113	938	22,465	41,855
Shiloh NMP	387,816	-	14,371	13,362	202	4,033	7,844
Sitka NHP	186,864	-	4,058	4,010	49	1,483	2,645
*Sleeping Bear Dunes NL	1,348,304	129,973	132,774	129,244	2,288	52,893	102,846
Springfield Armory NHS	16,161	-	1,112	1,034	14	438	800

Table A-1. Local-Level Impacts of NPS Visitor Spending on Local Economies by Park, 2011 (continued)

Park Unit	Public Use Data		Visitor Spending 2011		Impacts of Non-local Visitor Spending		
	2011 Recreation Visits	2011 Overnight Stays	All Visitors ($000's)	Non-local Visitors ($000's)	Jobs	Labor Income ($000's)	Value Added ($000's)
Statue of Liberty NM	3,749,982	-	174,607	157,217	2,009	79,828	137,508
Steamtown NHS	111,725	-	4,140	3,850	59	1,529	2,759
Stones River NB	187,208	-	9,911	9,215	143	4,716	7,784
Sunset Crater Volcano NM	185,265	-	9,808	9,119	121	2,986	5,514
Tallgrass Prairie NPRES	17,893	-	901	854	14	225	433
Thaddeus Kosciuszko NMEM	1,949	-	134	125	2	67	111
Theodore Roosevelt Birthplace NHS	6,537	-	450	418	5	216	358
Theodore Roosevelt Inaugural NHS	17,107	-	1,177	1,095	15	416	840
Theodore Roosevelt Island Park	137,690	-	9,476	8,811	95	3,743	6,225
Theodore Roosevelt NP	563,407	21,518	28,318	26,881	431	8,784	15,313
Thomas Edison NHP	55,284	-	3,805	3,538	40	1,830	3,024
Thomas Jefferson MEM	1,945,696	-	66,580	60,829	676	27,736	46,400
Thomas Stone NHS	6,351	-	437	406	4	173	287
Timpanogos Cave NM	96,965	-	6,673	6,205	100	2,856	4,840
Timucuan EHP	1,028,922	-	56,265	43,836	617	19,121	33,487
Tonto NM	53,426	-	2,828	2,630	40	1,279	2,227
Tumacacori NHP	33,740	-	1,250	1,163	16	426	783
Tuskegee Airmen NHS	16,244	-	860	800	13	303	523
Tuskegee Institute NHS	23,288	-	1,233	1,146	18	435	749
Tuzigoot NM	101,104	-	5,352	4,977	75	2,441	4,234
Ulysses S. Grant NHS	35,664	-	2,454	2,282	31	1,209	2,086
Upper Delaware S&RR	270,390	-	8,636	7,538	89	2,182	4,207
*Valley Forge NHP	1,303,046	2,000	49,497	35,127	560	21,595	34,786
Vanderbilt Mansion NHS	367,680	-	5,761	3,363	39	1,025	2,023
Vicksburg NMP	796,035	-	42,141	39,182	589	16,080	27,139
Vietnam Veterans MEM	4,020,127	-	137,566	125,682	1,397	57,307	95,869
*Virgin Islands NP	442,414	57,741	58,649	58,649	1,086	21,565	40,139
Voyageurs NP	177,184	65,465	8,972	8,593	137	2,993	5,566
Walnut Canyon NM	125,003	-	6,618	6,153	82	2,015	3,721
War in the Pacific NHP	482,391	-	17,876	16,621	245	4,892	9,380
Washington Monument	430,153	-	14,720	13,448	150	6,132	10,258
Washita Battlefield NHS	10,995	-	456	428	7	110	222
Weir Farm NHS	22,415	-	1,543	1,434	16	692	1,161
Whiskeytown NRA	761,710	43,713	33,980	29,683	386	8,906	18,157
White House	570,057	-	19,507	17,822	198	8,126	13,594
White Sands NM	428,924	2,185	15,812	15,500	230	5,053	9,091
Whitman Mission NHS	57,611	-	2,135	1,985	28	601	1,143
William Howard Taft NHS	21,141	-	1,455	1,353	22	646	1,053
Wilson's Creek NB	192,865	-	10,210	9,493	156	3,689	6,705
Wind Cave NP	538,394	3,054	51,506	51,381	890	19,661	34,288
Wolf Trap NP for the Performing Arts	425,177	-	29,261	27,206	292	11,558	19,222
*Women's Rights NHP	25,426	-	740	740	7	173	334
World War II Memorial	3,752,172	-	128,397	117,305	1,304	53,487	89,479
World War II Valor in the Pacific NM	1,694,896	-	71,109	63,623	735	24,117	42,948
Wrangell-St. Elias NP & PRES	65,225	-	3,110	3,110	44	1,174	2,123

Table A-1. Local-Level Impacts of NPS Visitor Spending on Local Economies by Park, 2011 (continued)

Park Unit	Public Use Data		Visitor Spending 2011		Impacts of Non-local Visitor Spending		
	2011 Recreation Visits	2011 Overnight Stays	All Visitors ($000's)	Non-local Visitors ($000's)	Jobs	Labor Income ($000's)	Value Added ($000's)
Wright Brothers NMEM	445,455	-	16,507	15,348	223	5,800	10,491
Wupatki NM	216,165	-	11,444	10,640	141	3,484	6,434
*Yellowstone NP	3,394,326	1,280,978	332,975	332,975	5,041	133,534	227,947
*Yosemite NP	3,951,393	1,630,610	379,116	374,136	5,003	128,202	251,573
Yukon-Charley Rivers NPRES	1,718	6,774	1,966	1,966	21	670	1,217
*Zion NP	2,825,505	312,608	138,697	137,403	2,286	51,416	98,433

* For these parks, results are based on a visitor survey at the designated park. For other parks, visitor characteristics and spending averages are adapted from national averages for each park type, adjusted for surrounding populations and spending opportunities.

Notes: Non-local visitors live outside a roughly 60-mile radius of the park. Jobs include part-time and full-time jobs with seasonal jobs adjusted to an annual basis. Impacts include direct and secondary effects of visitor spending on the local economy. Labor income covers wages and salaries, payroll benefits, and incomes of sole proprietors in the local region. Value added includes labor income, profits and rents, and indirect business taxes.

Table A-2. State-Level Impacts of NPS Visitor Spending on State Economies by State, 2011

State	Non-local Visitor Spending ($ Millions)	Jobs from Non-local Visitor Spending	Labor Income from Non-local Visitor Spending ($ Millions)	Value-added from Non-local Visitor Spending ($ Millions)
Alaska	237	4,138	116	200
Alabama	19	315	8	13
Arkansas	140	2,364	53	92
American Samoa	1	12	0[a]	1
Arizona	737	12,499	381	671
California	1,192	17,978	690	1,224
Colorado	319	4,621	148	266
Connecticut	1	19	1	1
District of Columbia	1,025	8,852	404	684
Florida	608	9,818	320	561
Georgia	241	3,592	108	189
Guam	17	268	8	14
Hawaii	259	3,113	104	187
Iowa	12	195	5	8
Idaho	24	379	8	15
Illinois	16	253	9	16
Indiana	54	826	20	35
Kansas	4	67	2	3
Kentucky	85	1,400	36	62
Louisiana	28	429	12	21
Massachusetts	432	6,917	179	307
Maryland	145	2,025	65	115
Maine	183	2,555	97	169
Michigan	159	2,875	82	148
Minnesota	37	665	19	33
Missouri	158	2,468	67	116
Mississippi	101	1,471	35	61
Montana	279	4,492	107	190
North Carolina	725	11,915	323	560
North Dakota	28	478	11	18
Nebraska	13	227	5	9
New Hampshire	1	20	1	1
New Jersey	117	1,807	63	113
New Mexico	98	1,479	36	63
Nevada	162	2,045	67	116
New York	341	3,998	159	274
Ohio	52	862	22	39
Oklahoma	14	177	5	9
Oregon	54	915	26	45
Pennsylvania	325	5,358	161	280
Puerto Rico	61	980	29	50
Rhode Island	3	45	1	2
South Carolina	48	704	18	31
South Dakota	160	2,576	54	93
Tennessee	530	8,847	261	452
Texas	177	2,798	91	164
Utah	693	11,240	336	565

Table A-2. State-Level Impacts of NPS Visitor Spending on State Economies by State, 2011 (continued)

State	Non-local Visitor Spending ($ Millions)	Jobs from Non-local Visitor Spending	Labor Income from Non-local Visitor Spending ($ Millions)	Value-added from Non-local Visitor Spending ($ Millions)
Virginia	541	8,116	237	417
Virgin Islands	65	1,236	37	63
Vermont	1	22	1	1
Washington	261	3,827	121	215
Wisconsin	24	455	12	19
West Virginia	60	869	21	36
Wyoming	621	9,098	222	397

[a] $0.35 million for labor income

Table A-3. Regional-Level Impacts of NPS Visitor Spending on Regional Economies by Region, 2011

Region	Non-local Visitor Spending ($ Millions)	Jobs from Non-local Visitor Spending	Labor Income from Non-local Visitor Spending ($ Millions)	Value-added from Non-local Visitor Spending ($ Millions)
Alaska Region	237	4,138	116	200
Intermountain Region	2,885	48,326	1,569	2,811
Midwest Region	854	15,630	462	810
National Capital Region	1,209	15,225	587	984
Northeast Region	1,847	28,802	1,071	1,873
Pacific West Region	2,022	30,612	1,144	2,026
Southeast Region	2,631	44,944	1,397	2,461

Table A-4. Allocations to States for Multi-State Parks

Park	State	Share
Assateague Island NS	MD	33%
Assateague Island NS	VA	67%
Bighorn Canyon NRA	WY	46%
Bighorn Canyon NRA	MT	54%
Big South Fork NRRA	KY	41%
Big South Fork NRRA	TN	59%
Blue Ridge Parkway	VA	38%
Blue Ridge Parkway	NC	62%
Chickamauga & Chattanooga NMP	GA	50%
Chickamauga & Chattanooga NMP	TN	50%
Chesapeake & Ohio Canal NHP	WV	6%
Chesapeake & Ohio Canal NHP	MD	9%
Chesapeake & Ohio Canal NHP	DC	85%
Cumberland Gap NHP	KY	93%
Cumberland Gap NHP	VA	7%
Delaware Water Gap NRA	PA	29%
Delaware Water Gap NRA	NJ	71%
Dinosaur NM	UT	26%
Dinosaur NM	CO	74%
Gateway NRA	NJ	20%
Gateway NRA	NY	80%
Glen Canyon NRA	AZ	8%
Glen Canyon NRA	UT	92%
Great Smoky Mountains NP	NC	44%
Great Smoky Mountains NP	TN	56%
Gulf Islands Nat Seashore	MS	25%
Gulf Islands Nat Seashore	FL	75%
Hovenweep NM	CO	44%
Hovenweep NM	UT	56%
Lake Mead NRA	AZ	25%
Lake Mead NRA	NV	75%
Natchez Trace Parkway	AL	7%
Natchez Trace Parkway	TN	13%
Natchez Trace Parkway	MS	80%
National capital Parks East	MD	10%
National capital Parks East	DC	90%
Saint Croix Nat scenic river	MN	50%
Saint Croix Nat scenic river	WI	50%
Upper Delaware SRR	NY	50%
Upper Delaware SRR	PA	50%
Yellowstone NP	WY	49%
Yellowstone NP	MT	51%

The Department of the Interior protects and manages the nation's natural resources and cultural heritage; provides scientific and other information about those resources; and honors its special responsibilities to American Indians, Alaska Natives, and affiliated Island Communities.